DO YOU ENJOY

Keto diet guide to Easy Low-Carb Recipes for Busy or Lazy Food Lovers Who Want to Save Time, Cook Food Slowly, and Burn Fat Fast

BY

SANDRA THOMPSON

Content

introduction

With the Instant Keto, you can use it to create golden-brown crunchy fried dishes, but also to roast, bake, and reheat yesterday's leftovers to perfection. In essence, your Instant Vortex Keto is a mini convection oven with some extra features. You'll be able to cook food in your keto that you'd usually pop into the oven or even the microwave.

How it works is straightforward. There's a heating element that creates veryhot air which is then moved around by a fan. The two main keto cooking methods are dry heat (frying) and wet heat (steaming or braising).

As you can see, the keto is a revolutionary appliance, and you won't have to sacrifice your culinary creativity. I've experimented with air frying the strangest foods, and I'm hardly ever disappointed. Fried strawberries, anyone?

Before we get to the recipes, I'm going to walk you through everything youneed to know about your Instant Vortex Keto, as well as cooking dos and don'ts.

Let's get started so that you can get cooking!

Cabbage and Red Onion Dahl With Buckwheat

Preparation time: 20 minutes -
Cooking time: 30 minutes -
Servings: 1
7.5-ounces hulled buckwheat
1.50ounces of curly cabbage

Vegetable broth
1 Tomato pulp
2 spoons of extra virgin olive oil
Red onion
Basil
Chopped chili pepper
Water
Pepper
Salt
1. Into a kettle, pour the water, add the oil and, to the fire, wait until it boils and
add the broth. Then turn off the heat. Meanwhile, wash the cauliflower, cut the
florets into small pieces and drain them. Chop the shallot finely enough. Pour the
buckwheat in a colander and rinse it under running water.
2. In another saucepan (large) pour two full spoons of oil, add the chopped

shallot, the mince for sautéing and fry it on a soft flame, often mixing to prevent
it from sticking to the pot. When the onion is transparent and dried, add the
buckwheat and toast it for a few minutes, mixing without letting it stick to the
bottom of the pot. Then add the tomato pulp, broth, chopped basil, chopped red
pepper, and mix, then add the cauliflower florets.
3. Cook the Buckwheat and cauliflower soup for 30 minutes, covering the pan
with a lid and on low heat, occasionally stirring so as not to stick the buckwheat
to the pan. If necessary, season with salt. After cooking, serve the buckwheat

and cauliflower soup with freshly ground pepper. If you like (and if you are not
vegan, vegetarian or lactose intolerant), you could also add some grated pecorino
cheese. Your buckwheat and cauliflower soup is ready!

Nutrition: Calories: 120, Sodium: 23 mg, Dietary Fiber: 2.4 g, Total Fat: 2.1 g,
Total Carbs: 1.3 g, Protein: 10.3 g.

Mushroom and Tofu Scramble

Preparation time: 10 minutes -
Cooking time: 20 minutes -
Servings: 2

7 ounces of extra firm tofu

2 teaspoon turmeric powder

1 teaspoon black pepper

1.50ounces of kale, roughly chopped

2 teaspoon extra virgin olive oil

1.5 ounces of red onion, thinly sliced

1 Thai chilies, thinly sliced

100g mushrooms, thinly sliced

4 tablespoons parsley, finely
chopped

1. To help it drain, cover the tofu in paper towels and put something heavy on
top.
2. Mix the turmeric with a little water until you achieve a light paste.
3. Steam the kale for 2 to 3 minutes.
4. Heat the olive oil over medium heat in a frying pan until hot but not smoky,
add the onion, chili, and mushrooms and fry for 2 to 3 minutes until they have
started to brown and soften.
5. Crumble the tofu and return to the pan into bite-size bits, pour the turmeric
paste over the tofu, and mix thoroughly. Add the black pepper and stir. Cook
over medium heat for 2 to 3 minutes, so the spices are cooked through and the
tofu has started to brown.

6. Attach the kale and continue cooking for another minute, over medium heat.

Finally, blend well, add the parsley, and serve.

Nutrition: Calories: 123 Sodium: 36 mg Dietary Fiber: 2.4 g Total Fat: 4.7 g

Total Carbs: 16.3 g Protein: 1.3 g

Kale Scramble

Preparation time: 10 minutes -
Cooking time: 6 minutes - Total
time: 16
minutes - Servings: 2
4 eggs
1/8 teaspoon ground turmeric
Salt and ground black pepper, to
taste
1 tablespoon water
2 teaspoons olive oil
1 cup fresh kale, tough ribs removed
and chopped

1. In a bowl, add the eggs, turmeric, salt, black pepper, and water and with a
whisk, beat until foamy.
2. In a wok, over medium heat, heat the oil.
3. Add the egg mixture and stir to combine.
4. Reduce the heat to medium-low right away and cook for about 1– 2 minutes,
stirring frequently.
5. Stir in the kale and cook for 3 to 4 minutes or so, stirring frequently.
6. Remove from the heat and serve immediately.

Nutrition: Calories: 183 Sodium: 35 mg Dietary Fiber: 2.4 g Total Fat: 4.1 g
Total Carbs: 16.8 g Protein: 1.6 g

Miso and Tofu With Sesame Glaze and Sautéed Vegetables in a Pan With Ginger and Chili

Preparation time: 20 minutes -
Cooking time: 10 minutes -
Servings: 1

2 teaspoons of extra virgin olive oil
7 ounces of mushrooms (enoki or champignon)
½ carrot, peeled and cut into julienne strips
1 red chili peppers, sliced
1 tablespoon of fresh ginger
Cabbage or spinach
Onion
Miso paste
125 g of tofu

1. In a large pan, heat the oil and add the mushrooms and carrot to it. Quickly

cook the vegetables for 1minute or as long as they are tender, add the chili, the
ginger and cook for 10 seconds.

2. Add the cabbage or spinach and ì onions in the pan and cook until the leaves
are slightly wilted. Remove them from the pans and divide them into two bowls.

3. Bring 700 ml of water to the boiling point in a large saucepan. Mix the miso
with a few teaspoons of water in a small bowl and add it to the pot. Stir to mix
and still incorporate miso if necessary. Divide the drained and diced tofu into the
bowls and cover with the miso broth. Add tamari or soy sauce and serve
immediately.

Nutrition: Calories: 114, Sodium: 7.3 mg, Dietary Fiber: 2.4 g, Total Fat: 2.1 g,
Total Carbs: 1.3 g, Protein: 5.3 g.

Turkey With Cauliflower Couscous

Preparation time: 20 minutes -
Cooking time: 50 minutes -
Servings: 1
3 ounces of turkey
2-ounce g of cauliflower
2 ounces of red onion
1 teaspoon fresh ginger
1 pepper Bird's Eye
1 clove of garlic
3 tablespoons of extra virgin olive oil
2 teaspoons of turmeric

1.3 ounces of dried tomatoes
0.3ounces parsley
Dried sage to taste
1 tablespoon of capers
1/4 of fresh lemon juice
1. Blend the raw cauliflower tops
and cook them in a teaspoon of
extra virgin
olive oil, garlic, red onion, chili
pepper, ginger, and a teaspoon of
turmeric.
2. Leave to flavor on the fire for a
minute, then add the chopped sun-
dried
tomatoes and 5 g of parsley. Season
the turkey slice with a teaspoon of
extra
virgin olive oil, the dried sage and
cook it in another teaspoon of extra
virgin
olive oil. Once ready, season with a
tablespoon of capers, 1/4 of lemon
juice, 5 g

of parsley, a tablespoon of water and add the cauliflower.

Nutrition: Calories: 114, Sodium: 7.3 mg, Dietary Fiber: 2.4 g, Total Fat: 2.1 g,
Total Carbs: 1.3 g, Protein: 5.3 g.

Oriental Prawns With Buckwheat

Preparation time: 20 minutes -
Cooking time: 20 minutes -
Servings: 1
3 ounces of shrimps
1 spoon of turmeric
1 spoon of extra-virgin oil
1.3 ounces of grain spaghetti
Cooking water
Salt
1 clove of garlic
Bird's Eye chili

1 spoon of ginger
Red onion
3 ounces of celery
1.3 ounces of green beans
1.7 ounces of kale
Broth

1. Cook for 2-3 minutes the peeled prawns with 1 teaspoon of turmeric and 1
teaspoon of extra virgin olive oil. Boil the buckwheat noodles in salt-free water,
drain and set aside.

2. Fry with another teaspoon of extra virgin olive oil, 1 clove of garlic, 1 Bird's
Eye chili and 1 teaspoon of finely chopped fresh ginger, 20 g of red onion and
40 g of sliced celery, 75 g of chopped green beans, 50 g of curly kale roughly
chopped.

3. Add 100 ml of broth and bring to a boil, letting it simmer until the vegetables
are cooked and soft. Add the prawns, spaghetti, and 5 g of celery leaves, bring to
the boil, and serve.

Nutrition: Calories: 114, Sodium: 7.3 mg, Dietary Fiber: 2.4 g, Total Fat: 2.1 g,
Total Carbs: 1.3 g, Protein: 5.3 g.

Blueberry Banana Pancakes

Preparation time: 10 minutes -
Cooking time: 10 minutes -
Servings: 1
3 bananas
3 eggs
75 g rolled oats
A pinch of salt
1 teaspoon baking powder
¾ cup of blueberries (fresh or
frozen)

1. To complete this recipe, you will need to do the following:

2. Put your oats into a blender or food processor and pulse until you have created
an oat flour.

3. In your food processor or blender, add in everything but the blueberries. Pulse
it together for roughly 2 minutes until it is well combined and you have a nice,
smooth batter.

4. Pour the batter into a large mixing bowl and gently add in the blueberries,
folding them in rather than mixing it up. Make sure that you do not overmix.

5. Wait 10 minutes, allowing the baking powder to activate.

6. Heat a medium-high frying pan and add a tiny amount of oil or butter to the

surface so that the pancake does not stick. Scoop in the blueberry banana batter

to the size desired and allowed it to fry until the bottom is golden brown and

ready to flip.

7. Flip and cook the other side until also golden brown.

Nutrition: Calories: 495 Sodium: 32 mg Dietary Fiber: 1.4 g Total Fat: 2.6 g

Total Carbs: 12.3 g Protein: 1.3 g

Breakfast Chocolate Muffins

Preparation time: 10 minutes -
Cooking time: 30 minutes -
Servings: 1

Almond paste

Banana (Blackberry)

1 Egg

1 Teaspoon vanilla extract

1/2 teaspoon tartar yeast

100 grams of chocolate chips

1. To prepare a baking tray made of paper or silicone muffins, preheat the oven

to 200 ° C.

2. Put all ingredients (except optional chocolate chips) in a food processor and
mix it in a smooth, sticky dough.

3. Optional: add and mix chocolate bars

4. Optional: add and incorporate chocolate bars

5. Place the dough in a muffin pan and bake until golden, then cook for about
12-15 minutes.

Nutrition: Calories: 205 Sodium: 32 mg Dietary Fiber: 1.5 g Total Fat: 5.1 g
Total Carbs: 16.4 g Protein: 1.3 g

21. Cauliflower Couscous

Preparation time: 20 minutes -
Cooking time: 10 minutes -
Servings: 1

28-ounces cauliflower

7 dried tomatoes

1 tablespoon of capers

1 anchovy in oil
2 tablespoons of pitted Taggiasca olives
1 clove of garlic
7 ounces of marinated anchovies
Fresh oregano
Extra virgin olive oil
1. To prepare the cauliflower couscous, remove the leaves and remove the
florets. Rinse the couscous under running freshwater, dab them with kitchen
paper to dry them and blend them, a little at a time, in a food processor and
transfer the granules obtained in a clean bowl.
2. Let the dried tomatoes soak in lukewarm water for half an hour, then squeeze
them, dab them with paper towels and cut them into thin strips. Drain the capers

and chop half of them with a knife. Coarsely chop also half of the olives. Peel

the garlic and use the palm of your hand to mash it. In a large pan, heat a little

oil. Fry the garlic with the capers (chopped and whole), the anchovy, and the

chopped olives. Also, add the sliced tomatoes over high heat.

3. Pour the cauliflower grains and stir in with a little water (about half a glass:

the cauliflower must remain crunchy), always on high heat, and stir. Add salt,

turn off the heat and add the anchovies marinated in fillets, the remaining olives,

a little fresh oregano leaves and a round of raw oil.

4. Serve the cauliflower couscous, hot or cold, depending on your taste.

Nutrition: Calories: 114, Sodium: 7.3 mg, Dietary Fiber: 2.4 g, Total Fat: 2.1 g,
Total Carbs: 1.3 g, Protein: 5.3 g.

Turkey Escalopes With Sage, Parsley, and Capers

Preparation time: 20 minutes -
Cooking time: 10 minutes -
Servings: 1
8 slices of turkey
Half white onion
1 large sprig of parsley
A few fresh sage leaves or a nice
pinch of the dried one
Olive oil to taste
Salt

Capers

Flour

1. Cover the turkey slices with flour once at the time, shake them slightly to
remove excess flour. Wash parsley, sage, and finely chop them with a knife, add
the capers. Finely chop the onion, heat up 2 tablespoons of oil in a pan, add the
onion, fry 1 minute, add 2 tablespoons of water, lower the heat, cover and cook
the onion, add 3 tablespoons of oil, raise the heat, put on the heat the slices of
turkey in the pan, brown them on both sides, salt.

2. One minute before turning off the heat, sprinkle the slices with the chopped
sage and parsley with capers. Serve with the sauce made from the pan.

Nutrition: Calories: 120, Sodium: 23 mg, Dietary Fiber: 2.4 g, Total Fat: 2.1 g,
Total Carbs: 1.3 g, Protein: 10.3 g.

Green Omelet

Preparation Time: 5 Minutes -
Cooking Time: 35 Minutes -
Servings: 1
1 tsp of olive oil
1 shallot peeled and finely chopped
2 large eggs
Salt and freshly ground black
pepper A handful of parsley, finely
chopped A handful of rocket
Heat the oil in a large frying pan,
over medium-low heat. Add the
shallot and
gently fry for about 5 minutes.
Increase the heat and cook for two
more minutes.
In a cup or bowl, whisk the eggs;
distribute the shallot in the pan then
add in the
eggs. Evenly distribute the eggs by
tipping over the pan on all sides.
Cook for

about a minute before lifting the sides and allowing the runny eggs to move to
the base of the pan.
Sprinkle rocket leaves and parsley on top and season with pepper and salt to
taste.
When the base is just starting to brown, tip it onto a plate and serve right away.
Nutrition Facts: Calories 221 kcal, Fat 28 g, Carbohydrate 10.6 g, Protein 9.5 g

Apple Blackcurrant Compote Pancakes

Preparation time: 5 minutes - Cooking time: 15 minutes - Servings: 4

For the compote:

3s of water 2s caster sugar

120 grams blackcurrants, washed and stalks removed

For The Apple Pancakes:

2 teaspoons light olive oil 2 egg whites 300 ml semi-skimmed milk 2 apples, cut into small pieces

Pinch of salt

2s of caster sugar

1 teaspoon of baking powder 125 grams plain flour

75 grams porridge oats

In a small pan, add the blackcurrants, water and sugar. Bring it to a boil and let it simmer for 10 to 15 minutes.

In a large bowl, place the flour, oats, baking powder, salt and caster sugar, mix well.

Add in the apple, stir and gently fold in semi-skimmed milk until mixture is smooth.

Beat the egg whites until firm peaks are formed, then gently whisk them into the mixture of flour. Pour batter into a jug.

Heat half teaspoon of oil over medium-high heat in a non-stick frying pan. Add about 1/4 of the batter into the pan. Cook pancake until golden brown on both sides. Drizzle the blackcurrant compote.

Nutrition: Calories: 337 Net carbs: 40 g Fat: 9.82g Fiber: 6.2 g Protein: 32g

Blueberry Oats Pancakes

Preparation time: 5 minutes -
Cooking time: 5 minutes - Servings:
4

225 grams blueberries
¼ teaspoon salt
2 teaspoon baking powder
150 grams rolled oats
6 eggs
6 bananas

Pulse the rolled oats for 1 minute in a (dry) high-speed blender to form oat flour.

Add in the eggs, bananas, salt and baking powder and process for 2 minutes until
it forms a smooth batter.

Pour the batter into a big bowl and add the blueberries, stirring gently. Let sit for
at least 10 minutes to activate the baking powder.

Over a medium high heat, add a big spoonful of butter to the frying pan. Scoop the batter and cook until nicely golden underneath. Flip pancake and cook
the other side.
Nutrition: Calories: 494 Net carbs: 68 g Fat: 11.3g Fiber: 6.2 g Protein: 22.23g

Muesli Yoghurt Breakfast

Preparation time: 3 minutes - Cooking time: 0 minutes - Servings: 1

100g plain Greek, coconut or soya yoghurt 100g hulled and chopped strawberries

10g cocoa nibs

15g chopped walnuts

40g pitted and chopped Medjool dates 15g coconut flakes

10g buckwheat puffs 20g buckwheat flakes

Mix together the cocoa nibs, buckwheat flakes, coconut flakes, buckwheat puffs,

Medjool dates and walnuts. Add the yoghurt and strawberries.

Nutrition: Calories: 368 Net carbs: 49g Fat: 11.5g Fiber: 7.4g Protein: 16.54g

Omelette Fold

Preparation time: 3 minutes -
Cooking time: 5 minutes - Servings:
1

1 teaspoon extra virgin olive oil
5 grams thinly sliced parsley 35
grams thinly sliced red chicory 3
medium eggs
50 grams streaky bacon, cut into
thin strips
Cook the bacon strips in hot non-
stick frying pan over high heat until
crispy.
Remove and drain any excess fat on
a kitchen paper.
Beat the eggs in a small bowl and
mix with the parsley and chicory.
Mix the
drained bacon through the egg
mixture.
In a non-stick pan, heat the olive oil;
add the mixture. Cook until
omelette is set.

Loose the omelette around the edges with a spatula and fold into half-moon.

Nutrition: Calories: 471 Net carbs: 3.3g Fat: 38.72g Fiber: 1.5g Protein: 27g

Rice Pudding

Preparation Time: 5 minutes -
Cooking Time: 15 minutes -
Servings: 5

1 cup of brown rice
2 cups coconut milk, unsweetened
1 teaspoon cinnamon
1 teaspoon ginger
1/3 teaspoon thyme
1/3 cup almonds
2 tablespoon honey
1 teaspoon lemon zest

1. Pour the coconut milk into a saucepan and heat until low.
2. Add the brown rice and stir the mixture carefully.
3. Close the lid and cook the brown rice over medium heat for 10 minutes.
4. Meanwhile, crush the almonds and combine them with the lemon zest, thyme, ginger, and cinnamon.

5. Sprinkle the brown rice with the almond mixture and stir it carefully.
6. Close the lid and cook the dish for 5 minutes.
7. Remove it from the saucepan when the pudding is cooked, and transfer it to a
large bowl.
8. Add the honey and stir the pudding.
9. Serve it immediately.
Nutrition: Calories: 423, Fat: 27.1g, Total Carbs: 43.3g, Sugars: 10.4g, Protein:
6.5g

Creamy Millet

Preparation Time: 10 minutes -
Cooking Time: 15 minutes -
Servings: 8

2 cups millet
1 cup almond milk, unsweetened
1 cup of water
1 cup coconut milk, unsweetened
1 teaspoon cinnamon
½ teaspoon ground ginger
¼ teaspoon salt
1 tablespoon chia seeds
1 tablespoon cashew butter
4 oz. Parmesan cheese, grated

1. Combine the coconut milk, almond milk, and water together in the saucepan.
2. Stir the liquid gently and add millet.
3. Mix carefully and close the lid.
4. Cook the millet on the medium heat for 5 minutes.

5. Sprinkle the porridge with the cinnamon, ground ginger, salt, and chia seeds.

6. Carefully stir the mixture with a spoon and proceed to cook for 5 minutes
more on medium heat.

7. Add the cashew butter and cook the millet for 5 minutes.

8. Remove the millet from the heat and transfer it to serving bowls.

9. Sprinkle the dish with the grated cheese.

Nutrition: Calories: 384, Fat: 19.8g, Total Carbs: 42.9g, Sugars: 3.6g, Protein:
11.7g

Apple Muffins

Preparation Time: 10 minutes -
Cooking Time: 15 minutes -
Servings: 5

2 eggs

1 cup oat flour

½ teaspoon salt

2 tablespoon stevia

3 apples, washed and peeled

½ cup skim milk

1 tablespoon olive oil

½ teaspoon baking soda

1 teaspoon apple cider vinegar

1. In the mixing bowl, beat and whisk the eggs well.
2. Add the skim milk, salt, baking soda, stevia, and apple cider vinegar.
3. Stir the mixture carefully.
4. Grate the apples and add the grated mixture in the egg mixture.
5. Stir it carefully and add the oat flour.

6. Add the olive oil and blend into a smooth batter
7. Preheat the oven to 350 F.
8. Fill each muffin from halfway with the batter and place the muffins in the oven.
9. Cook the dish for 15 minutes.
10. Remove the cooked muffins from the oven.
11. Cool the cooked muffins well and serve them.

Nutrition: Calories: 20, Fat: 6.0g, Total Carbs: 32.4g, Sugars: 15.3g, Protein:11.7g

Mushroom Frittata

Preparation Time: 10 minutes -
Cooking Time: 20 minutes -
Servings: 5
8 oz. shiitake mushrooms
1 teaspoon salt
1 cup broccoli
7 eggs
5 oz. Parmesan cheese
1 tablespoon olive oil
½ teaspoon ground ginger
5 garlic cloves
1 teaspoon oregano
1 teaspoon basil
1 teaspoon cilantro
½cuplow-
Fat milk
1. Wash the shiitake mushrooms
well and chop them.
2. Chop the broccoli and combine it
with the mushrooms in a mixing
bowl.
3. In a separate bowl, beat the eggs.

4. Sprinkle the egg mixture with the cilantro, basil, oregano, and ground ginger.
Stir it well.
5. Add the low-Fat milk and broccoli. Stir the egg mixture well.
6. Peel the garlic cloves and mince them.
7. Add minced garlic in the egg mixture and stir it gently.
8. Preheat the oven to 350 F.
9. Spray a deep pan with olive oil
10. Into the pan, pour the egg mixture and put it in the preheated oven.
11. Cook the frittata for 20 minutes.
12. Remove it from the oven when the dish is baked, and cool slightly.
Nutrition: Calories: 250, Fat: 15.5g, Total Carbs: 11.5g, Sugars: 3.7g, Protein: 19.2g

Homemade Granola Bowl

Preparation Time: 10 minutes -
Cooking Time: 20 minutes -
Servings: 6

3 tablespoons pumpkin seeds
1 tablespoon coconut oil
1 teaspoon sunflower seeds
¼ cup almonds
1 cup raw oats
3 tablespoons sesame seeds
5 tablespoons honey
2 cups almond milk, unsweetened

1. Combine the pumpkin seeds, sunflower seeds, almonds, and sesame seeds together.
2. Crush the mixture well and add raw oats.
3. Add the honey and coconut oil.
4. Stir the mixture carefully until you get a smooth mix.
5. Preheat the oven to 350 F.

6. Cover the tray with parchment and transfer the seed mixture onto the tray.
Flatten it well.
7. In the preheated oven, bring the tray in and cook for 20 minutes.
8. When the mixture is cooked, remove it from the oven and chill well.
9. Separate the mixture into small pieces and put in serving bowls.
10. Add the almond milk and mix up the dish.
Nutrition: Calories: 381, Fat: 28.5g, Total Carbs: 30.8g, Sugars: 17.4g,
Protein: 6.4g

Steak with Veggies

Preparation Time: 15 minutes -
Cooking Time: 12 minutes -
Servings: 4
2 tablespoons coconut oil
4 garlic cloves, minced
1-pound beef sirloin steak, cut into
bite-sized pieces Ground black
pepper, as required
1½ cups carrots, peeled and cut into
matchsticks 1½ cups fresh kale,

tough ribs removed and chopped 3 tablespoons tamari

1. Melt the coconut oil in a wok and sauté the garlic over medium heat for
approximately 1 minute.
2. Add the beef and black pepper and stir to combine.
3. Increase the heat to medium-high and cook for about 3-4 minutes or until
browned from all sides.
4. Add the carrot, kale and tamari and cook for about 4-5 minutes.
5. Remove from the heat and serve hot.

Nutrition: Calories 311 Total Fat 13.8 g Saturated Fat 8.6 g Cholesterol 101 mg
Sodium 700 mg Total Carbs 8.4 g Fiber 1.6 g Sugar 2.3 g Protein 37.1 g

Shrimp with Veggies

Preparation Time: 15 minutes - Cooking Time: 8 minutes - Servings: 5

For Sauce:

1 tablespoon fresh ginger, grated
2 garlic cloves, minced
3 tablespoons low-sodium soy sauce
1 tablespoon red wine vinegar
1 teaspoon brown sugar
¼ teaspoon red pepper flakes, crushed

For Shrimp Mixture:

3 tablespoons olive oil

1½ pounds medium shrimp, peeled and deveined

12 ounces broccoli florets

8 ounces, carrot, peeled and sliced

1. For sauce: in a bowl, place all the ingredients and beat until well combined.

Set aside.

2. In a large wok, heat oil over medium-high heat and cook the shrimp for about

2 minutes, stirring occasionally.

3. Add the broccoli and carrot and cook about 3-4 minutes, stirring frequently.

4. Stir in the sauce mixture and cook for about 1-2 minutes.

Nutrition: Calories 298 Total Fat 10.7 g Saturated Fat 1.3 g Cholesterol 305 mg

Sodium 882 mg Total Carbs 7 g Fiber 2g Sugar 2.4 g Protein 45.5 g

Chickpeas with Swiss Chard

Preparation Time: 15 minutes -
Cooking Time: 12 minutes -
Servings: 4

2 tablespoon olive oil
2 garlic cloves, sliced thinly
1 large tomato, chopped finely
2 bunches fresh Swiss chard, trimmed
1 (18-ounce) can chickpeas, drained and rinsed

Salt and ground black pepper, as required

¼ cup of water

1 tablespoon fresh lemon juice

2 tablespoons fresh parsley, chopped

1. Heat the oil in a large nonstick wok over medium heat and sauté the garlic for

about 1 minute.

2. Add the tomato and cook for about 2-3 minutes, crushing with the back of the

spoon.

3. Stir in remaining ingredients except for the lemon juice and parsley and cook

for about 5-7 minutes.

4. Drizzle with the lemon juice and remove from the heat.

5. Serve hot with the garnishing of parsley.

Nutrition: Calories 217 Total Fat 8.3 g Saturated Fat 1 g Cholesterol 0 mg Sodium 171 mg Total Carbs 26.2 g Fiber 6.6 g Sugar 1.8 g Protein 8.8 g

Buckwheat Noodles with Chicken

Preparation Time: 20 minutes -
Cooking Time: 25 minutes -
Servings: 2
½ cup broccoli florets
½ cup fresh green beans, trimmed
and sliced
1 cup fresh kale, tough ribs removed
and chopped
5 ounces buckwheat noodles
1 tablespoon coconut oil
1 red onion, chopped finely

1 (6-ounce) boneless, skinless chicken breast, cubed
2 garlic cloves, chopped finely
3 tablespoons low-sodium soy sauce

1. In a medium pan of the boiling water, add the broccoli and green beans and
cook for about 4-5 minutes.
2. Add the kale and cook for about 1-2 minutes.
3. Drain the vegetables and transfer into a large bowl. Set aside.
4. In another pan of the lightly salted boiling water, cook the soba noodles for
about 5 minutes.
5. Drain the noodles well and then, rinse under cold running water. Set aside.
6. Meanwhile, in a large wok, melt the coconut oil over medium heat and sauté
the onion for about 2-3 minutes.

7. Add the cubes of chicken and cook for approximately 5-6 minutes.
8. Add the garlic, soy sauce and a little splash of water and cook for about 2-3
minutes, stirring frequently.
9. Add the cooked vegetables and noodles and cook for about 1-2 minutes,
tossing frequently.
10. Serve hot with the garnishing of sesame seeds.
Nutrition: Calories 463 Total Fat 11.7 g Saturated Fat 5.9 g Cholesterol 54 mg
Sodium 1000 mg Total Carbs 58.9 g Fiber 7.1 g Sugar 4.6 g Protein 22.5 g

Spicy Sesame & Edamame Noodles

Preparation Time: 5 minutes -
Cooking Time: 15 minutes -
Servings: 2
100 g Blue Dragon Whole-wheat
Noodles
100 g vegetable 'noodles'
2 tbsp. groundnut or coconut oil
2 shallots, peeled and finely sliced
2 tsp. 'lazy' garlic
2 tsp. ginger puree
1 red chili, sliced
3 tbsp. sesame seeds
100 g edamame beans, podded
2 tbsp. sesame oil
2 tbsp. Blue Dragon soy sauce
Handful fresh coriander, roughly
chopped
Juice of 1 lime
1. For 4 minutes, boil the noodles,
then drain and set aside. Cook the
vegetable

noodles according to the Directions: and add the rest of the noodles.

2. In a big pan or kettle heat the oil and add garlic, ginger and pepper. Cook for 2

minutes and then add sesame seeds and bean sprouts. Cook for another 2

minutes, stir and stir to make sure nothing sticks to the bottom of the pot.

3. Pour the noodles and the noodles into the pan and cook for 2 minutes.

4. Turn off the heat, then add sesame oil, soy sauce and lemon juice and mix.

Serve with scattered coriander.

Nutrition: Calories 230 Carbs 25g Fat 13g Protein 4g

Triple Berry Millet Bake

This breakfast bake is full of blueberries, raspberries, and strawberries, which
are then complemented with walnuts? Enjoy it alone or with shavings of dark
chocolate over the top.

kilocalories Per Individual Serving: 342

The Number of Servings: 8

Time to prepare/Cook: 70 minutes

Millet - 1.5 cups

Soy milk, unsweetened - 2 cups

Water - 1 cup

Date sugar - .5 cup

Vanilla extract - 2 teaspoons

Sea salt - .25 teaspoon

Cinnamon - .5 teaspoon

Walnuts, chopped - 1 cup

Blueberries, thawed if frozen - 12 ounces

Strawberries, sliced, thawed if frozen - 8 ounces
Raspberries, thawed if frozen - 8 ounces

1. Set your oven to Fahrenheit three-hundred and seventy-five degrees and
prepare a glass 9-inch by thirteen-inch baking dish.

2. In a large kitchen bowl, whisk together the soy milk, water, millet, date sugar,
cinnamon, sea salt, and vanilla extract. Pour the mixture into the prepared pan.

3. Sprinkle the berries and almonds evenly over the top of the pan, and then use
a spatula or spoon to slightly press the nuts down into the mixture.

4. Bake the millet until hot and bubbling, about one hour. Remove the millet

bake from the oven and allow it to sit for fifteen minutes before serving.

Green Shakshuka

This shakshuka is a twist on the
original, with kale, zucchini,
Brussels sprouts,
and more, to give you a filling and
healthy start to your day.
kilocalories Per Individual Serving:
364
The Number of Servings: 3
Time to Prepare/Cook: 17 minutes
Zucchini, grated - 1
Brussels sprouts, finely sliced or
shaved - 9 ounces
Red onion, diced - 1
Olive oil - 2 tablespoons
Eggs - 5
Parsley, chopped - .25 cup
Kale, chopped - 2 cups
Sea salt - .5 teaspoon
Cumin - 1 teaspoon
Avocado, sliced - 1

1. In large steel, the skillet salutes the red onion in the olive oil until it becomes
slightly transparent, about three minutes. Add in the minced garlic and cook the
onion/garlic mixture for an additional minute.
2. Add the Brussels sprouts to the skillet containing the onion and garlic, and
cook it for four to five minutes until softened, stirring frequently. Stir in the
spices and zucchini, cooking for an additional minute.
3. Stir the kale into the skillet and continue to stir until it begins to wilt. Reduce
the heat to low.
4. Using a spatula flatten the shakshuka mixture in the skillet and create five

small wells for the eggs to next in. Crack an egg into each of the shakshuka
wells and cover the skillet with a lid to steam the eggs until they fit your liking.
5. Top the dish off with the parsley and avocado, serving immediately.

Kale and Butternut Bowls

You can easily make the vegetable portion of this dish ahead of time and store it
in the fridge or freezer. This will encourage you to reheat it in the mornings
easily and serve it with little effort alongside an egg.

kilocalories Per Individual Serving: 324

The Number of Servings: 4

Time to Prepare/Cook: 60 minutes

Red onion, diced - 1

Butternut s q uash, seeds removed and cut into quarters - 1

Kale, chopped - 3 cups

Garlic, minced - 2 cloves

Extra virgin olive oil - 1 tablespoon

Oregano, dried - 1 teaspoon

Cinnamon - .25 teaspoon

Turmeric powder - .5 teaspoon

Sea salt - 1 teaspoon

Avocado, sliced - 1

Eggs - 4

Parsley, chopped - .25 cup

Black pepper, ground - .25 teaspoon

1. Set the oven to Fahrenheit four-hundred and twenty-five degrees. Place the
butternut squash on a pan upside-down so that the skin side is facing upward.
Roast the butternut squash until it is fork-tender, about twenty-five to thirty
minutes.

2. Allow the butternut squash to cool enough to handle easily, and then peel the
skin off with your hands. Slice the butternut squash into bite-size cubes.

3. Heat the extra virgin olive oil in a large skillet over medium heat and saute the

onion for about five minutes until it is translucent. Add in the kale, garlic, and
seasonings, cooking until the kale is wilted. Add in the butternut squash.
4. Divide the skillet mixture between four serving bowls and top each one with
an egg cooked to your choice, sliced avocado, and parsley.

Egg Casserole

This casserole is full of flavor from your favorite breakfast sausage, vegetables
and fresh herbs. You can easily make this at the beginning of the week, and then
store it in the fridge for a quick and easy go-to meal.

kilocalories Per Individual Serving: 309

The Number of Servings: 6

Time to Prepare/Cook: 40 minutes

Eggs - 10

Breakfast sausage - 1 pound

Button mushrooms, sliced - 2 cups

Roma tomatoes, seeded and diced - 3

Red onion, thinly sliced - 1

Kale, chopped - 2 cups

Basil, chopped - 1 tablespoon

Parsley, chopped - 2 tablespoons

Sea salt - 1.5 teaspoons

1. Set your oven to Fahrenheit three-hundred and fifty degrees and prepare a
nine-inch by thirteen-inch baking dish.
2. In a skillet over medium-high brown, your breakfast sausage until fully
cooked, draining off any excess fat.
3. Into the skillet with the breakfast sausage, add the mushrooms, allowing them
to saute until tender, about five to seven minutes. Add in the sea salt and
remaining vegetables, cooking for an additional two to three minutes until just
slightly tender.
4. Transfer the vegetable sausage mixture to the prepared pan.
5. Whisk together the eggs in a large bowl, ensuring the whites fully break down

into the yolks. Pour the eggs over the breakfast sausage and mix vegetables, then
placing it in the oven to roast until cooked through, about twenty-five to thirty
minutes.

Vegan Tofu Omelet

This vegan omelet uses tofu to create an egg-like texture, and black salt to give it
an egg-like flavor. You can buy black salt online and at specialty stores. If you
can't find black salt, you can replace it with regular sea salt, but know it won't
have the same egg-like flavor.
kilocalories Per Individual Serving: 276
The Number of Servings: 1
Time to Prepare/Cook: 15 minutes
Silken tofu - 6 ounces Tahini - 1 teaspoon (optional)
Cornstarch - 1 tablespoon
Nutritional yeast - 1 tablespoon
Soy milk, unsweetened - 1 tablespoon
Turmeric, ground - .125 teaspoon
Onion powder - .25 teaspoon

Sea salt - .25 teaspoon
Smoked paprika - .125 teaspoon
(optional)
Black salt - .25 teaspoon
Kale, chopped - .5 cup
Button mushrooms, sliced - .25 cup
Onion, diced - 2 tablespoons
Garlic, minced - 1 clove
Extra virgin olive oil - 1 tablespoon,
dived
1. Into a blender, add the tofu,
tahini, cornstarch, yeast, soy milk,
turmeric, onion
powder, smoked paprika, and bath
salts.Pulse on high until fully
blended with
the mixture.
2. In a skillet, add half of the olive
oil along with the vegetables and
garlic. Saute
until they become tender, about five
minutes over medium heat.

3. Meanwhile, add the remaining half of the olive oil to a non-stick medium
skillet over medium-high heat. Allow this skillet to preheat while you cook the
vegetables until it is very hot. Once hot, pour the tofu batter into the skillet,
slightly tilting the pan so that the egg forms a circular shape. You can use a
spoon to smooth out the top.

4. Sprinkle the cooked vegetables over the tofu "egg" and reduce the heat of the
skillet to medium-low. Cover the skillet with a lid, allowing it to cook three to
five minutes until the tofu "egg" is set and the edges have dried. You can use a
spatula to lightly lift the edges of the omelet and ensure it is fully set. The

coloring should be golden with some browned spots.

5. When ready, loosen the omelet by lifting it with the spatula and then flip one
side over the other. Transfer the tofu omelet to a plate and enjoy while warm.

Grapefruit & Celery Blast

1 grapefruit, peeled
2 stalks of celery
50g (2oz) kale
½ teaspoon matcha powder
The Number of Servings: 1, 71
calories per serving
1. Place all the ingredients into a
blender with enough water to cover
them and
blitz until smooth.

Tropical Chocolate Delight

1 mango, peeled & de-stoned
75g (3oz) fresh pineapple, chopped
50g (2oz) kale
25g (1oz) rocket
1 tablespoon 100% cocoa powder or
cacao nibs 150mls (5fl oz) coconut
milk
The Number of Servings: 1, 427
calories per serving
1. Place all of the ingredients into a
blender and blitz until smooth.
When it
seems too thick, you should add a
little water.

Walnut & Spiced Apple Tonic

6 walnuts halves
1 apple, cored
1 banana
½ teaspoon matcha powder
½ teaspoon cinnamon
Pinch of ground nutmeg
The Number of Servings: 1, 272
calories per serving
1. Place all of the ingredients into a
blender and add sufficient water to
cover
them. Blitz until smooth and
creamy.

Sweet Rocket (Arugula) Boost

25g (1oz) fresh rocket (arugula) leaves
75g (3oz) kale
1 apple
1 carrot
1 tablespoon fresh parsley
Juice of 1 lime
The Number of Servings: 1, 113 calories per serving
1. Place all of the ingredients into a blender with enough water to cover and
process until smooth.

Banana & Ginger Snap

2.5cm (1 inch) chunk of fresh ginger, peeled

1 banana

1 large carrot

1 apple, cored

½ stick of celery

¼ level teaspoon turmeric powder

The Number of Servings: 1, 166 calories per serving

1. Place all the ingredients into a blender with just enough water to cover them.

2. Process until smooth

87. Chocolate, Strawberry & Coconut Crush

100mls (3½fl oz) coconut milk

100g (3½oz) strawberries

1 banana

1 tablespoon 100% cocoa powder or cacao nibs

1 teaspoon matcha powder

The Number of Servings: 1, 324 calories per serving
1. Toss all of the ingredients into a blender and process them to a creamy
consistency. Add a little additional water if you need to thin it out a little.

Chocolate Berry Blend

50g (2oz) kale
50g (2oz) blueberries
50g (2oz) strawberries
1 banana
1 tablespoon 100% cocoa powder or
cacao nibs 200mls (7fl oz)
unsweetened soya milk
The Number of Servings: 1, 241
calories per serving
1. Place all of the ingredients into a
blender with enough water to cover
them
and process until smooth.

Cranberry & Kale Crush

75g (3oz) strawberries
50g (2oz) kale
120mls (4fl oz) unsweetened cranberry juice 1 teaspoon chia seeds
½ teaspoon matcha powder
The Number of Servings: 1, 71 calories per serving
1. Place all of the ingredients into a blender and process until smooth. Add some
crushed ice and a mint leaf or two for a refreshing drink.

Poached Eggs & Rocket (Arugula)

2 eggs

25g (1oz) fresh rocket (arugula)

1 teaspoon olive oil

Sea salt

Freshly ground black pepper

The Number of Servings: 1, 178 calories per serving

1. Scatter the rocket (arugula) leaves onto a plate and drizzle the olive oil over

them. Bring a shallow pan of water to the boil, Put the eggs in and cook until the

whites are strong. Serve the eggs on top of the rocket and season with salt and

pepper.

Strawberry Buckwheat Pancakes

100g (3½oz) strawberries, chopped
100g (3½ oz) buckwheat flour
1 egg
250mls (8fl oz) milk
1 teaspoon olive oil
1 teaspoon olive oil for frying
Freshly squeezed juice of 1 orange
The Number of Servings: 4, 175
calories per serving
1. Pour the milk into a bowl and mix
in the egg and a teaspoon of olive
oil. Sift
in the flour to the liquid mixture
until smooth and creamy. Allow it to
rest for 15
minutes. Heat a little oil in a pan
and pour in a quarter of the mixture
(or to the
size you prefer.) Sprinkle in a
quarter of the strawberries into the
batter—Cook

for around 2 minutes on each side.
Serve hot with a drizzle of orange
juice. You
could try experimenting with other
berries such as blueberries and
blackberries.

Strawberry & Nut Granola

200g (7oz) oats
250g (9oz) buckwheat flakes
100g (3½ oz) walnuts, chopped
100g (3½ oz) almonds, chopped
100g (3½ oz) dried strawberries
1½ teaspoons ground ginger
1½ teaspoons ground cinnamon
120mls (4fl oz) olive oil
2 tablespoon honey
The Number of Servings: 12, 391 calories per serving
1. Combine the oats, buckwheat flakes, nuts, ginger and cinnamon. In a
saucepan, warm the oil and honey,. Stir until the honey has melted. Pour the
warm oil into the dry ingredients and mix well. Spread the mixture out on a large

baking tray (or two) and bake in the oven at 150C (300F) for around 50 minutes
until the granola is golden. Allow it to cool. Add in the dried berries. Store in anairtight container until ready to use. Can be served with yogurt, milk or even dry
as a handy snack.

Chilled Strawberry & Walnut Porridge

100g (3½ oz) strawberries
50g (2oz) rolled oats
4 walnut halves, chopped
1 teaspoon chia seeds
200mls (7fl oz) unsweetened soya
milk 100ml (3½ fl oz) water
The Number of Servings: 1, 384
calories
1. Place the strawberries, oats, soya
milk and water into a blender and
process
until smooth. Stir in the chia seeds
and mix well. Chill in the fridge
overnight
and serve in the morning with a
sprinkling of chopped walnuts. It's
simple and
delicious.

Chili con Carne

Preparation Time: 5 minutes -
Cooking Time: 30 minutes -
Servings: 3
450g (1lb) lean minced beef
400g (14oz) chopped tomatoes
200g (7oz) red kidney beans
2 tbsp tomato purée
2 cloves of garlic, crushed
2 red onions, chopped
2 bird's eye chilies, finely chopped
1 red pepper (bell pepper), chopped
1 stick of celery, finely chopped
1 tbsp cumin

1 tbsp turmeric

1 tbsp cocoa powder

400ml (14 oz) beef stock (broth)

175ml (6fl oz) red wine

1 tbsp olive oil

In a large saucepan, heat the oil, add the onion and cook for 5 minutes.

Add in the garlic, celery, chili, turmeric, and cumin and cook for 2 minutes

before adding then meat then cook for another 5 minutes.

Pour in the stock (broth), red wine, tomatoes, tomato purée, red pepper (bell

pepper), kidney beans and cocoa powder.

Nutrition: Calories: 320 Fat: 21 g Carbohydrates: 8 g

Protein: 24 g Fiber: 4 g

Tofu Thai Curry

Preparation Time: 5 minutes -
Cooking Time: 30 minutes -
Servings: 3
400g (14oz) tofu, diced
200g (7oz) sugar snap peas
5cm (2-inch) chunk fresh ginger
root, peeled and finely chopped 2
red
onions, chopped
2 cloves of garlic, crushed
2 bird's eye chilies
2 tbsp tomato puree

1 stalk of lemongrass, inner stalks only
1 tbsp fresh coriander (cilantro), chopped
1 tsp cumin
300ml (½ pint) coconut milk
200ml (7fl oz) vegetable stock (broth)
1 tbsp virgin olive oil
juice of 1 lime

In a frying pan, heat the oil, add the onion and cook for 4 minutes.

Add in the chilies, cumin, ginger, and garlic and cook for 2 minutes.

Add the tomato puree, lemongrass, sugar-snap peas, lime juice and tofu and
cook for 2 minutes.

Pour in the stock (broth), coconut milk and coriander (cilantro) and simmer for 5
minutes.

Serve with brown rice or buckwheat and a handful of rockets (arugula) leaves on
the side.

Nutrition: Calories: 412 Fat: 30 g Carbohydrates: 27 g
Protein: 14 g Fiber: 5 g

Roast Balsamic Vegetables

4 tomatoes, chopped
2 red onions, chopped
3 sweet potatoes, peeled and chopped
100g (3½ oz) red chicory (or if unavailable, use yellow)
100g (3½ oz) kale, finely chopped
300g (11oz) potatoes, peeled and chopped
5 stalks of celery, chopped
1 bird's eye chili, deseeded and finely chopped
2 tbsp fresh parsley, chopped

2 tbsp fresh coriander (cilantro)
chopped
3 tbsp olive oil
2 tbsp balsamic vinegar
1 tsp mustard
Sea salt
Freshly ground black pepper
Place the olive oil, balsamic,
mustard, parsley, and coriander
(cilantro) into a
bowl and mix well.
Toss all the remaining ingredients
into the dressing and season with
salt and
pepper.
Transfer the vegetables to an
ovenproof dish and cook in the oven
at 200C/400F
for 45 minutes.
Nutrition: Calories: 70 Fat:0 g
Carbohydrates: 8 g Protein: 2 g
Fiber: 2 g

Fruit & Nut Yogurt Crunch

100g (3½ oz) plain Greek yogurt
50g (2oz) strawberries, chopped
6 walnut halves, chopped
The sprinkling of cocoa powder
The Number of Servings: 1, 296 calories
1. Stir half of the chopped strawberries into the yogurt. Using a glass, place a
layer of yogurt with a sprinkling of strawberries and walnuts, followed by
another layer of the same until you reach the top of the glass.
2. Garnish with walnuts pieces and a dusting of cocoa powder.

Cheesy Baked Eggs

4 large eggs
75g (3oz) cheese, grated
25g (1oz) fresh rocket (arugula)
leaves, finely chopped
1 tablespoon parsley
½ teaspoon ground turmeric
1 tablespoon olive oil
The Number of Servings: 4, 198
calories per serving
1. Grease each ramekin dish with a
little olive oil. Divide the rocket
(arugula)
between the ramekin dishes then
break an egg into each one. Sprinkle
a little
parsley and turmeric on top then
sprinkle on the cheese. In a
preheated oven,
place the ramekins at220C/425F for
15 minutes, until the eggs are set
and the
cheese is bubbling.

Tofu and Curry

Preparation Time: 5 minutes -
Cooking Time: 36 minutes -
Servings: 4

8 oz dried lentils (red preferably)
1 cup boiling water
1 cup frozen edamame (soy) beans
7 oz (½ of most packages) firm tofu,
chopped into cubes
2 tomatoes, chopped
1 lime juices
5-6 kale leaves, stalks removed and
torn
1 large onion, chopped
4 cloves garlic, peeled and grated
1 large chunk of ginger, grated
½ red chili pepper, deseeded (use
less if too much)
½ tsp ground turmeric
¼ tsp cayenne pepper
1 tsp paprika
½ tsp ground cumin 1 tsp salt
1 tbsp olive oil

Add the onion, sauté in the oil for few minutes then add the chili, garlic, and
ginger for a bit longer until wilted but not burned.
Add the seasonings, then the lentils and stir

Nutrition: Calories: 250 Fat:5 g Carbohydrates: 15 g
Protein: 28 g Fiber: 1 g

Chicken and Bean Casserole

Preparation Time: 5 minutes -
Cooking Time: 40 minutes -
Servings: 3
400g (14oz) chopped tomatoes
400g (14oz) tinned cannellini beans
or haricot beans
8 chicken thighs, skin removed
2 carrots, peeled and finely chopped
2 red onions, chopped
4 sticks of celery

4 large mushrooms
2 red peppers (bell peppers), deseeded and chopped
1 clove of garlic
2 tbsp soy sauce
1 tbsp olive oil
1.75 liters (3 pints) chicken stock (broth)

Heat the olive oil in a saucepan, put in garlic and onions and cook for 5 minutes.

Add in the chicken and cook for 5 minutes then add the carrots, cannellini beans, celery, red peppers (bell peppers) and mushrooms.

Pour in the stock (broth) soy sauce and tomatoes.

Bring it to the boil, reduce the heat and simmer for 45 minutes.

Serve with rice or new potatoes.

Nutrition: Calories: 32

Moroccan Chicken Casserole

CateCanCook.blogspot.com

Preparation Time: 5 minutes -
Cooking Time: 20 minutes -
Servings: 3
250g (9oz) tinned chickpeas
(garbanzo beans) drained
4 chicken breasts, cubed
4 Medjool dates halved
6 dried apricots, halved
1 red onion, sliced

1 carrot, chopped
1 tsp ground cumin
1 tsp ground cinnamon
1 tsp ground turmeric
1 bird's eye chili, chopped
600ml (1 pint) chicken stock (broth)
25g (1oz) corn flour
60ml (2fl oz) water
2 tbsp fresh coriander

Place the chicken, chickpeas (garbanzo beans), onion, carrot, chili, cumin, turmeric, cinnamon, and stock (broth) into a large saucepan.

Bring it to the boil, reduce the heat and simmer for 25 minutes.

Add in the dates and apricots and simmer for 10 minutes.

In a cup, mix the corn flour with the water until it becomes a smooth paste.

Pour the mixture into the saucepan and stir until it thickens.

Add in the coriander (cilantro) and mix well.

Nutrition: Calories: 423 Fat: 12 g Carbohydrates: 0 g Protein: 39 g Fiber: 0 g